The Ramsbottoms at Home

Barbara Mitchelhill

Stanley Thornes (Publishers) Ltd

Originally published in 1988 by Hutchinson Education

Reprinted 1990 by
Stanley Thornes (Publishers) Ltd
Old Station Drive
Leckhampton
CHELTENHAM GL53 0DN

British Library Cataloguing in Publication Data

Milchelhill, Barbara
The Ramsbottoms at home
1. English language – Readers – For slow learning students
I. Title II. Series
428'.6'2

ISBN 0 7487 0362 4

Cover illustration by Simon Rees
Cover design by Ned Hoste

Set in Linotron Rockwell
Printed and bound in Great Britain at
Martin's of Berwick

Contents

A Good Warm Fire

4 parts:
Dad, Eric (the son), Snarl (the family dog), Mum.

Sound effects (FX):
Wind (made by blowing into an empty yoghurt carton).
Door closing (use the classroom door or a desk lid).

Scene	A small house, miles from anywhere.
FX	*Wind (Until the door is shut).*
Dad	Put another log on the fire, son.
Eric	I can't, Dad, that was our last one.
Dad	Then go and chop a tree down.
Eric	I chopped the last one down on Saturday. There aren't any trees left.
Dad	No trees, eh? I remember when I was a lad you could look out of that window and see trees for miles and miles.
Eric	There's just miles and miles of nothing now. What are we going to put on the fire?
Dad	Stand up.

Eric	What for?
Dad	We'll burn your chair.
Eric	You can't do that! I'll have nothing to sit on.
Dad	When I was a lad, we didn't have chairs.
Eric	What did you sit on?
Dad	We had a sack stuffed with straw. Just one between fifteen of us. Life was hard then.
Eric	It's not so easy now.
Dad	Don't sit there arguing – stand up and give me your chair.
Eric	Can't we wait till Mum gets back?
Dad	Where's she gone?
Eric	To get some coal. She'll be back soon.
Dad	All right then. Just as long as she's not too long. That fire's nearly out.
Eric	I know. It's freezing in here.
Dad	Freezing? . . . Freezing? When I was a lad it was so cold in our kitchen that there was ice on top of our porridge.
Eric	It might help if we shut that door. I'm cold. [*Shuts door*]
Dad	You're soft you young ones. When I was

your age, it was so cold in the bedroom that I had to sleep with my head under the blanket.

Eric Why did you do that?

Dad Frostbite, son.
Noses have dropped off with frostbite in our family.
It was a horrible sight. I've seen them lying there on the blanket in the morning.

Eric Oh, you did have blankets then?

Dad Not exactly blankets. No. We were too poor.

Eric What did you have?

Dad Dog-hair covers.

Eric Dog-hair covers? What were they?

Dad We had a great, long-haired dog and every day we had to brush him and collect the hair. Then your grandmother would spin the hair to make thread. All through the day and night that poor woman would spin till her fingers had blisters the size of door knobs.

Eric And what did she do then?

Dad She'd weave the thread into blankets.

Eric Were they warm?

Dad They were warm all right – but very itchy.

Eric	Did the hair tickle?
Dad	Not the hair . . . the fleas.
Eric	Ugh . . . not dog fleas.
Dad	Full of them.
Eric	Couldn't you wash the blankets?
Dad	No soap, son. You can't afford soap when you've got nineteen children to feed.
Eric	I thought you said there were only fifteen?
Dad	Fifteen . . . nineteen . . . I lose count.
Eric	Well, I'm fed up with being poor. When I'm a man, I'm going out into the big wide world to make my fortune.
Dad	But, Eric, you're twenty-three years old now.
Snarl	Woof . . . wooof . . . woooof.
Eric	Listen, our Snarl's barking. I bet Mum's back. [*Door opens*]
FX	*Wind (Until door is shut).*
Mum	It's me.
Eric	Hello, Mum.
Dad	Got the coal, love?

Mum Yes, it's here.

Snarl Grrrrrrr . . . grrrrr.

Mum Just get Snarl off my skirt, will you, love? . . . and help me lift the sack off my back.

Dad Go on, Eric. Give your mother a hand.

Eric All right, then.

Snarl Grrrrrrr . . .

Eric Get off, Snarl. Go and find a rabbit or something.

Snarl Woof . . . [*He leaves*]

[*Door closes*]

Mum I expect you're waiting for me to make you a nice fire.

Dad That's right, Doris. The boy and me were just sitting here looking forward to a bit of warmth.

Mum Well, it won't take long. I've got some lovely coal today. Look.

Eric Oh, come on, Mum. Keep piling it on.

Dad That's a lovely fire. It's coming on a treat. Where did you get the coal from, love?

Mum From Hinkley Bottom.

Eric Oh yes.

Mum I set off at seven o'clock this morning.

Dad I didn't hear you go.

Mum No, I didn't want to wake you.

Eric Which way did you go?

Mum Across Hemlock Edge, down Wendle Ridge, over Thor Beacon. . . .

Dad Nice day for it.

Mum . . . up Clumber Pass, along Pine Top and on to Hinkley Bottom mine.

Dad Oh Yes.

Mum Then I went down the mine shaft 400 feet . . . walked along the first tunnel for two miles . . . then I had to crawl the rest of the way till I came to the coal face and I got to work.

Dad I hope you didn't use my best pick, Doris.

Mum No of course not, love. I used that old kitchen knife you said I could have.

Dad That's all right then.

Mum So when I'd filled my sack I crawled back along the tunnel . . . back up the shaft

[*Dad and Eric begin to yawn noisily*]

Mum ... along Pine Top
... down Clumber Pass
... over Thor Beacon
... up Wendle Ridge
... across Hemlock Edge and back home.

Dad Well done, love. Very good.
You can come and sit with Eric and me and enjoy this lovely fire – just as soon as you've finished making our tea.

Mum If you don't mind, dear, I'll just rest my feet for a few minutes before I start cooking.

Dad Rest? In front of the fire?

Mum Yes. Just for five minutes. I'm really tired . . . zzzzzzzz.

Dad Do you know, Eric, your mother's always been a disappointment to me. A great disappointment.

Eric Has she, Dad? Why?

Dad Because she's all talk and no action.

Mum [*Snores growing louder*]

The Visitor

5 parts:
Snarl (the family dog), Dad, Eric (the son), Mum, the Visitor.

Scene	A small house, miles from anywhere.
Snarl	Woof . . . woof . . . woof . . . grrrrrr.
Dad	Is that our Snarl barking?
Eric	I think so.
Dad	What's he barking at?
Eric	Must have seen a rabbit.
Snarl	Woof . . . woof . . . woof . . . grrrrr.
Dad	Have a look out of the window, son. See what he's up to.
Eric	All right, Dad, I'll go.
Snarl	Woof . . . woof . . . grrrrrrr.
Eric	Hey, Dad, come and look at what Snarl's doing.
Dad	Can't you just tell me? I've got my feet up and I'm comfortable.

Eric Oh, Dad – you've got to see this. Come on, quick.

Dad You know, son, at my time of life I need rest.

Eric You've been resting since Monday.

Dad When you're my age you need lots and lots of rest.

Eric You're only forty-three years old and I'm only asking you to walk over to the window.

Snarl Woof . . . woof . . . grrrrrrr.

Dad Oh, all right, I'll come.

Snarl Woof . . . woof . . . woof . . . grrrrrr.

Dad Where is he? I can't see him.

Eric He's just behind that bush by the stream – look.

Dad Oh, yes. I see him now. Good heavens – what's he got? Oh no . . . It's not . . .

Eric It is.

Dad Not again.

Eric It looks like it.

Dad Oh, botheration. Your mother had better see this. Doris. Come here. Quick.

Mum In a minute, Arthur. I'm up to my elbows in pigs' trotters.

Dad Never mind your pigs' trotters. I want you to come now.

Snarl Woof . . . woof . . . woof . . . grrrrrr.

Mum Whatever is it?

Dad It's our Snarl. He's at it again.

Mum What . . . ? Where . . . ?

Eric Down the bottom of the path by that bush.

Mum That prickly one by the stream?

Dad That's it – he's right behind it.

Mum Oh, yes. I see him now. Good gracious me. What's he got? Oh no. It's not . . .

Eric and Dad It is.

Mum Not again.

Eric and Dad It looks like it.

Snarl Grrrrrrrrr . . . Woof . . . woof.

Visitor Help . . . get off . . . stop it.

Mum Well, I'm blowed. He has . . . Snarl has got the postman again.

Snarl Woof . . . woof . . . grrrrrrrr.

Visitor Ahhhhhhh . . . oooooooh.

Eric Don't you think we'd better help him?

Dad Our Snarl doesn't need any help.
He can manage very nicely by himself.

Eric Not Snarl – the postman.

Visitor Ahhhhhhh . . . oooooooh.

Eric He seems to be in quite a bit of pain.

Dad Well, if you think so, son. You and your mother go and drag our Snarl off him.
I'll go and get some beer.

Mum That's kind of you Arthur. I expect the poor chap will be glad of a drink.

Dad You daft so-and-so – I'm getting it for me.
My nerves are shattered with all this excitement.

Snarl Woof . . . woof . . . grrrrrr.

Eric Oh look. Our Snarl has let him go.

Mum I expect he's had enough fun for one day.
He'll have gone to look for somebody else to play with.

Visitor [*Groans*]

Eric The postman is doing well. He's managing to crawl up the path.

Mum His trousers are in a bit of a state. I bet his wife will be mad when he gets home.

Eric He's left his jacket behind.

Mum That was careless of him.

Eric Half of it is hanging on the bush and the rest of it is floating down the stream.

[*KNOCK, KNOCK*]

Mum Well, he's got to the front door.

Dad Yes, he has.

[*KNOCK, KNOCK, KNOCK*]

Mum It didn't take him long – and him with that bad leg.

[*KNOCK, KNOCK, KNOCK, KNOCK*]

Dad Open the door, son.

Eric Oh, all right, Dad.
[*Door opens*]

Eric Good morning.

Visitor Urrrrrrr . . . ahhhhh [*groans*].

Eric Can I help you?

Visitor I've . . . I've . . .

Eric You'll have to speak up.

Visitor I've got . . .

Mum What's he trying to say, son?

Eric I'm not sure. He seems a bit dazed.

Dad I'll speak to him.
[*Shouting*] What . . . do . . . you . . . want?

Visitor (*Spluttering*] I want to g . . .

Mum Wipe the mud out of his mouth, Eric, then we can tell what he's saying.

Eric Why do I get all the rotten jobs?

Dad Eric.

Eric Oh, all right, Dad.
[*Wipes the mud out of the postman's mouth*]

Visitor Ooooooooh . . . ahhhhhhh . . . ughhhhhhh.

Dad That's better. Now then – [*Loudly*] What . . . do . . . you . . . want?

Visitor [*Breathless and whispering*] I've . . . got . . . a . . . letter.

Mum Oh, fancy.

Dad A letter? We never get letters.

Visitor	I've come ... all the way ... from Gurney with it.
Mum	Nice place Gurney. We try to go there once a year, if we can.
Visitor	I've been walking for five ... long ... hours.
Mum	I like a nice walk myself.
Visitor	Five long hours in the wind and the snow and the rain.
Mum	Terrible weather we've been having lately.
Visitor	Five hours in the wind and the snow and the rain, with a hole in my left boot.
Eric	Fancy somebody sending us a letter.
Dad	Right then – where is it?
Visitor	[*Shakily*] It's in my bag. Just a minute and I'll get it for you.
Eric	He'll never get it out while his hands are shaking like that.
Dad	Come on – pull yourself together. Give me the letter.
Visitor	I'm trying ...
Dad	You're trying all right – very trying! Now will you hurry up and find my letter?
Visitor	I think I've got it. Yes, I have. Here it is Mr Baker.

Dad Baker? Baker? I'm not Baker. I'm Ramsbottom – Arthur Ramsbottom.

Visitor Do you mean I've come to the wrong house?

Dad You certainly have.

Visitor . . . and I've walked all that way for nothing?

Mum That's right.

Visitor Five hours in the wind and snow and rain . . .

Eric Yes.

Visitor . . . with a hole in my left boot . . .

Mum You want to get that boot mended.

Visitor . . . and been attacked by a dog?

Eric Our Snarl was only having a bit of fun.

Visitor And now I've got to walk all the way back to Gurney . . . five long miles in the . . .

Dad Don't start all that again.

Visitor But it's a long way – especially with a hole in my boot.

Mum You're right. It is a long way. But before you go . . .

Visitor [*Happily*] Yes?

Mum Would you mind waiting while I pop into the kitchen?

Visitor Are you going to make a cup of tea?

Mum No. I'm going to get my library books so that you can drop them in at the Gurney Public Library on your way back.

Visitor What?

Mum . . . and if they ask you to pay the fines, pretend you don't understand.

Eric It always works. They think Mum is stupid.

Visitor I can believe it – but I'm not stupid. I'm going.
[*Door bangs*]

Dad You know, Doris, things are not what they were, are they?

Mum They're not, Arthur.

Dad In the good old days, I've known our postman carry a dustbin full of rubbish all the way to Gurney just to make us happy.

Mum Just goes to show – no consideration these days. No consideration at all.

Leaving Home

4 parts:
Snarl (the family dog), Eric (the son), Mum, Dad.

Scene	A small house, miles from anywhere.
Snarl	[*Howls*]
Eric	It's no good, Snarl, you'll have to learn to wear a collar. Now . . . SIT.
Snarl	[*more howls*]
Mum	What's going on down there? Is that you, Eric?
Eric	No, it's our Snarl howling.
Mum	But why is he howling? What are you doing to him? Poor little thing.
Eric	He's not a poor little thing, Mum. He's the size of a donkey.
Mum	I'm coming down. I want to see what you're up to.
Snarl	[*Howls*]

Mum	Here's Mummy, my little one. What's the matter?
Eric	Nothing – I'm all right.
Mum	I wasn't talking to you, Eric. I was talking to our Snarl.
Snarl	[*Howls*]
Mum	There now . . . Mummy's here. No more nasty howling from my baby.
Eric	Snarl is not your baby. Mother. I am your baby, your only child, and I am leaving home.
Mum	What?
Eric	I am leaving home and taking the dog with me.
Mum	[*Bursts into tears*]
Snarl	[*Howls*]
Dad	What on earth is going on down here? Can't a man get a bit of rest? The racket you're making could waken the dead.
Eric	I've just told Mum I'm leaving home.
Mum	[*Sobs*]
Dad	Now then, Doris, don't upset yourself. He's a grown man.

Mum I know – but he's taking the dog with him. [*More sobs*]

Snarl [*Howls*]

Dad QUIET you two. Now, son, what's all this about leaving home?

Eric I'm going out into the world – just me and the dog. I'm going to find fame and fortune.

Mum Our Eric's never been the same since we took him to see that pantomime last Christmas.

Dad Fancy yourself as Dick Whittington, do you, son?

Eric Dick Whittington had a cat not a dog. And I'm not going to London.

Dad But this is your home, Eric. There have been Ramsbottoms at Craggy Top for hundreds of years. Why do you want to go now?

Eric Because I don't want to live the rest of my life in this rotten old house.

Mum Don't you talk like that, my lad. Be thankful you've got a roof over your head.

Eric But I haven't. If I think it's going to rain in the night, I have to go to sleep in my plastic mac.

Mum [*Sobs*]

Dad You never go without food.

Eric But I don't want porridge three times a day and pigs' trotters on Sunday. I want exciting things like chips and mushy peas . . . giant hamburgers and ice cream.

Dad Eh, son, those things are not for the likes of us.

Eric Well, I'm going to have all of those things one day. What's more, I'll have boots that don't let the rain in.

Dad You've got perfectly good plastic bags to put over yours.

Eric . . . and I want a coat with sleeves and buttons.

Mum Now you're really going too far, Eric. [*Sobs*]

Eric I want to buy things for you, too, Mum.

Mum Do you, son?

Eric I want to put glass in the windows . . .

Mum Oh lovely.

Eric . . . and tiles on the roof . . .

Dad Never.

Eric . . . and a new plastic bucket in the well.

Mum	Luxury.
Dad	But how are you going to pay for all of this?
Eric	I'm going to the big city.
Snarl	[*Howls*]
Dad	The big city? You don't mean Blundersfield, do you, son?
Mum	Oh no. Not Blundersfield. [*Sobs*]
Snarl	[*Whimpering*]
Eric	Yes, I'm going to find work in Blundersfield. I'm a man and I want to be rich and famous. One day you'll be proud of me.
Mum	I was proud of you the day you were born, Eric. I was proud of you the day you were three and you put on your first pair of Dad's cast-off trousers.
Eric	But that is just it, Mum. I don't want cast-off trousers. I want trousers of my own.
Dad	When I was a lad my trousers were handed down from my grandfather to my father and then to me. What's good enough for me is good enough for my son.
Eric	When I'm rich and famous, I'll buy you a pair of trousers, Dad.

Dad What's wrong with these? They're good for another twenty years.

Eric A coat then.

Dad No.

Eric A warm jumper to keep out the cold.

Dad I don't want one.

Eric Then I'll buy you as much beer as you can drink.

Dad Now you're talking, son. I'll help you pack.

Eric I know you'll be proud of me, Dad.

Dad 'Course I will. Let's find him some food, Mother, to help him on his way.

Mum Wrap it in a cloth for him.

Dad Like Dick Whittington, eh son?
Right – here we go.

Mum No, Arthur. Not porridge.
If you put porridge in a cloth, it will drip.

Dad Then have some bread and goose grease.

Eric Thanks, Dad.

Snarl [*Howls*]

Mum No, Snarl, it's not for you.

Dad Are you ready, son?

Eric I'm ready for anything.

Mum You've got a terrible long walk to Blundersfield.

Eric What's fifty-six miles. I'm strong and healthy.

Mum But there's the Trendle river to cross and it has a fearful current. Many a man has been swept to his death.

Eric Not Eric Ramsbottom. I will succeed where others have failed.

Dad There's Pie Crag to climb. Will you be able to manage it?

Eric Nothing can stop me now. I will climb the highest mountains and cross dangerous rivers. I will reach Blundersfield and make my fortune – or die from trying.
Poor I may be, but I am strong and brave.

Dad Then good-bye, son.

Eric Good-bye, Dad.

Mum [*Sobbing*] My baby – take care.

Eric I will, Mother. Come on, Snarl.

Snarl [*Howls*]

[*Door closes*]

Dad He's gone, Doris.

Mum They've both gone. [*Sobs*]

Dad Don't cry, love. He'll be back, one day.

Mum Yes, but when? [*Sobs*]

[*Knock at door*]

Dad Hello, son. That was quick – what happened?

Eric It started raining, Dad. I'm all wet.

Dad Oh . . . so you're not going to Blundersfield to make your fortune.

Eric No, Dad. The weather's not right for making fortunes today. I think I'll wait a bit. I don't like getting wet. It's bad for my chest.

Dad Very sensible.

Mum Yes, a true Ramsbottom. Welcome home, son. Welcome home.

A complete list of Spirals

Stories

Jim Alderson
Crash in the Jungle
The Witch Princess

Jan Carew
Death Comes to the Circus

Susan Duberley
The Ring

Keith Fletcher and Susan Duberley
Nightmare Lake

John Goodwin
Dead-end Job

Paul Groves
Not that I'm Work-shy
The Third Climber

Anita Jackson
The Actor
The Austin Seven
Bennet Manor
Dreams
The Ear
A Game of Life or Death
No Rent to Pay

Paul Jennings
Eye of Evil
Maggot

Margaret Loxton
The Dark Shadow

Patrick Nobes
Ghost Writer

Kevin Philbin
Summer of the Werewolf

John Townsend
Beware of the Morris Minor
Fame and Fortune
SOS

David Walke
Dollars in the Dust

Plays

Jan Carew
Computer Killer
No Entry
Time Loop

John Godfrey
When I Count to Three

Nigel Gray
An Earwig in the Ear

Paul Groves
Tell Me Where it Hurts

Barbara Mitchelhill
Punchlines
The Ramsbottoms at Home

Madeline Sotheby
Hard Time at Batwing Hall

John Townsend
Cheer and Groan
The End of the Line
Hanging by a Fred
The Lighthouse Keeper's Secret
Making a Splash
Murder at Muckleby Manor
Over and Out
Taking the Plunge

David Walke
The Bungle Gang Strike Again
The Good, the Bad and the Bungle
Package Holiday

Freedom in the Unknown